PENCILS

AND

STICKS

PENCILS

AND

STICKS

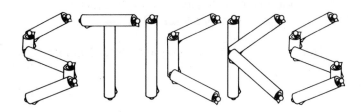

Scripture Word-Searches For LDS Families

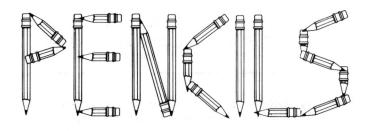

Joseph K. Kayne

Second Printing: September, 1995

International Standard Book Number:
0-88290-218-0

Horizon Publishers' Catalog and Order Number
2018

Printed and distributed
in the United States of America by

Horizon Publishers
& Distributors, Incorporated
P.O. Box 490 Bountiful, Utah 84011-0490

To My Children

Jhenene

David

Elena

Sylvia

Joseph

Michael

?

?

?

etc.

Introduction

How do you get a kid to use the scriptures and enjoy it?

How do you keep the family occupied on trips and use the scriptures at the same time?

How can you make a family home evening fun and enjoyable by using the scriptures?

How can you turn spare time into fun, scripture-learning time for anyone who can read? . . .

Do what we do—use this book of puzzles.

If your family is anything like our family, getting the members to use the scriptures for any reason is a task for the taskmaster. Let's face it; most people don't use the standard works as often as they should. For this reason I decided to find a way to make using the scriptures fun and enjoyable. My efforts have been successful in our stake, so I am passing them on to you. This is how it works:

T	B	O	L	Y	U	M	A	W	R	E	C	K	L
R	I	L	O	E	S	T	I	C	K	S	P	D	N
O	B	I	V	T	K	S	O	S	T	H	R	M	H
Y	L	V	E	B	D	S	C	R	I	P	T	U	R
S	E	E	V	O	S	N	I	A	T	R	U	C	T
P	M	R	M	T	R	E	L	I	E	E	V	O	L
P	R	I	M	A	R	Y	S	N	O	M	R	O	M

A block or configuration of letters will contain the clue words spelled forward, backward, vertically, horizontally, and diagonally.

The clue word must first be located by finding the passage of scripture in which it is contained. For example:

James 1:5—If any of you lack ______________.
Wisdom is the clue word. Locate wisdom in the puzzle block and circle it.

How about this one:

Exodus 26:7—And thou shall make ______________ of goats hair. The clue word is *curtains*. Locate curtains in the puzzle block and circle it. It's as simple as that.

You will find answers to each of the puzzles in the back of the book, but try to do them without looking at the answers. Consider the solving of each puzzle as a challenge to use the scriptures; to find in them the answers you will need.

Some of the puzzles will be more difficult than others to solve and these will require more study and research. To complete these puzzles can be an uplifting experience for you and your family.

We do not always have the scriptures handy when we need them, such as when taking short trips with the family. Puzzles are included which have the clue words listed.

It is my hope and prayer that many enjoyable and learning hours will be spent using this book.

Sincerely,

Joseph D. Kayne

A Word Of Advice

Don't be fooled!
Be sure of your spelling!

Contents

PLACES AND THINGS FROM THE BOOK OF MORMON

```
                     R N
                 L O E Y N E
             T R A M C K R O R Y
         S E G A U G N A L E Z C T F
     N O R I M K Z E O Z I F V I U O E F
 Y N E M E S H T E G I I D F Z L S L T F I Z
A B R E Z A H S T N E M R A G L U F I T U A E B E A
S E R I P R I T R E C U L F M T O L D S N F I S P L
E Z F F E K C O C K A T R I C E S G O L K E Z S P D
S F O P     I O R N O I T C U R T S E D     P A O R
O C P P         B E A U T I F O L T         A R C O
M O R E             S T S A E B             R B E W
C E C R                 O K                 B A S S
```

Campsite	Shazer	1 Nephi 16:13
Money	Lucre	Mosiah 29:40
Den	COCKatrices	2 Nephi 21:8
Weapon	Sword	Alma 2:1
Hunt	Beasts	Enos 3
Law	Moses	Jarom 11
Confounded	Language	Omni 22
Witnessed	record	Words of Mormon 1
Murderer	destruction	Helaman 1:9
Clothing	beautiful garments	Moroni 10:31
Poisonous	serpents	Ether 10:19
Metals (6)	gold	Mosiah 11:3
	Silver	
	Ziff	
	copper	
	Brass	
	Iron	

JESUS WAS:

```
                  O P
                U D E C
              H R Y E D R
            T E N R L G B U
          I H Z O D S U R E C
        W P B A P N A Z E U D I
      D E T P M E T L I D L O O F
    D H U D E K C O M Y N E T C G Y
  E S C Y P F B W R K T B Z P I S F B
V D I U M Z E D T N L O V E D P L Y O Z
O O D E Z I T P A B A P T I S G D I R Y N E
L O I Y L T R A N S F I G U R E D O M H E W O N
G R A C E A                         T R S H Y S
R E L I Y                             T H R E E
A P O E                                 E W O R
C E D                                     N E W
E N                                         O L
D                                             D
```

Luke 4:2, 4; 12 Tempted

John 19:1 Scourged

Mark 4:38 asleep

Matthew 3:13 baptized

Matthew 17:2 tranfigured

Matthew 26:24 betrayed

John 10:11 Shepard

John 3:18 begotten

Mark 15:13 crucified

John 9:38 worshipped

Mark 15:20 Mocked

Mark 15:39 Son of god

LAND AND WATER

```
                    O
                  S S C
                E R N B E
              K E A O A T A
            A V M B I Y S L N
          L I A C R T O E E J K
        B R L O R O A U A E B O N
      B O D Y E E O L N R M O U S O
    P A U U A A E K O U O T A L S H L
  N O Y N N I R K S S Y F I M G U I L S
H O N O T E T T S A E R L I T E I A A E T
I M D U I S N H L R D A M O T N M D K D R
L R M O F T A E S I M O R P R N U Q E N I
L O U M U A M A R S H Y E O A Y U O S O A
S M D E L S P R I N G S D N P A L T M P N
              T N O D I S D
              H I L L S E S
              S C O C E A N
```

Water	______________________________	Alma 17:26
Water	______________________________	1 Nephi 17:5
Land	______________________________	1 Nephi 17:5
Water	______________________________	1 Nephi 17:26
Water	______________________________	Alma 3:3
Water	______________________________	Mosiah 18:8
Land	______________________________	1 Nephi 2:20
Land	______________________________	Alma 6:8
Land	______________________________	1 Nephi 17:20
Land	______________________________	Alma 43:42
Land	______________________________	Alma 22:30
River	______________________________	1 Nephi 2:8

"ITES" OF THE BOOK OF MORMON

S E T I N A B A L A M A T I T E S S J E
A S E T I J I T R M E L I L S I E I O Z
M M I T O E S M J U T E A I T T L Z S E
I E A S Z E Y A I L I M E E I Z O T E K
T I E L T T R I T O A U S M J R A S P I
E P I I E E I S E N R E E O A E D E H E
H I T S D K E T I I O L T M C M I T I L
R O I I L T I T E T M I I I O I T I T I
M E T Z I O E T I E S T E T B T E H E T
T E M T R S Z O E S E E S E I E S P S E
S M I T H I T E S S E S T S T I T E I S
E H J A E I S H M A E L I T E S I N E I
B I S H O P I T E S B O R I S I T E S S

Jacob 1:13 (7) __________

Moroni 9:23 __________

Alma 25:29 (2) __________

12 DISCIPLES CHOSEN BY JESUS

```
        M             E
      K L I         Z T Z
    R H S U L     E I Z E I
  A Z A A Z K U K M E O D S J
M E I Y E H Y E O D T S E A O M
D A E N Z A I T E I A O K I H A
H Z T O H L H N M N I A I A N T
  K U H M Y I O O K M O A S O
    Z T O M A J Y H L T H Y
      N T N T I U Z T E S
      A Y E I H M Y M A O
      L Z M M N E N N Y M
          U O O O O P
          K T N J T A
          Y H E O Y P
              M H
              U N
              K H
            J O A S
          Z U I I H L
        K E D H M E U Z
        U D A P E M E E
          E S E R E K
            T N E N
              L J
```

3 Nephi 19:4

PLAIN AND PRECIOUS

A	G	A	R	M	A	G	E	D	O	D	L	A	R	E	M	E	R	E
N	A	N	O	S	L	A	G	I	D	O	R	P	I	E	A	T	O	M
Y	X	Y	N	N	O	N	Y	E	L	C	N	U	B	R	A	C	X	E
N	O	S	U	I	D	R	A	S	A	C	A	R	I	I	T	A	G	A
O	X	Y	X	I	N	O	B	M	A	S	D	M	S	H	X	Y	N	P
U	A	D	S	E	H	T	E	B	J	R	A	Z	A	P	O	T	D	R
I	S	Y	X	V	E	T	H	A	D	T	N	O	Z	P	Y	X	I	O
D	N	O	N	N	H	R	S	P	H	O	B	D	I	A	M	O	N	D
R	O	A	O	Y	T	P	R	A	D	P	E	P	U	S	Y	N	M	I
A	I	M	S	L	E	P	E	D	I	G	R	E	E	S	N	Y	T	G
S	P	T	I	R	I	A	E	M	T	M	Y	D	S	K	O	X	E	G
U	R	H	N	Y	X	G	B	S	U	P	L	C	C	O	R	R	N	A
I	O	Y	E	O	A	E	U	S	U	S	O	I	I	A	U	I	I	R
D	C	S	V	M	R	U	T	R	P	R	T	P	F	P	H	R	T	E
R	S	T	R	Y	M	E	P	U	E	S	R	A	O	T	P	A	Z	M
A	G	A	T	E	R	L	T	E	S	O	L	C	R	O	R	P	A	D
S	P	L	O	Z	E	P	O	T	C	B	P	A	C	D	O	I	N	A
P	V	E	N	I	S	E	N	S	Y	R	F	S	E	T	D	O	J	S

(PLAIN AND PRECIOUS)

City ______________________ Matt. 27:57

Battle ______________________ Rev. 16:14-16

Well of the oath ______________________ Gen. 21:31-32

Naval hospital ______________________ John 5:2

Breastplate stones (12) ______________________ Exod. 39:8-13

____

____

____

____

____

____

____

____

____

____

____

Sting ______________________ Deut. 8:15

Blood lines ______________________ Num. 1:18

Seed ______________________ Matt. 13:31

The uttermost ______________________ Matt. 5:26

Into ______________________ Matt. 6:6

Deer ______________________ Gen. 25:28

Of Judah ______________________ Ezek. 37:16

Color ______________________ Num. 4:13

MIRACLES

```
X                                         X
B A                                     S L
Y T N                                 N E C
H S P G                             A P R E
A E U Y E                         E R E D A
H B A B G L                     C O A U S R
T E E V A E S                 O S T T R E T
I A M T E R Y O G E N D E B A Y E I U S B H
B U A A H N A L A M B A D A Z D T E M P E R
A T N M Y E S B U I L N E C M L F M R O T S
T H U E S A E N I W Y I N S U E D E M L A C
P C E D D R S M T I M E D M G R S W A E T S
H A E T E E A R T S Y L I E H N E H N F G U
A R L E A R M                 C I E T B R H
R D I M D A                     A L W E A C
O A O P N                         H A Z G Y
E H N N                             S E E T
R S A                                 E H U
Y T                                     M E
X                                         X
```

Dan 3:26 — Three men in fiery furnace: ____________________

____

____

Daniel 6:16 — ____________________ cast into den of lions.

Exodus 16:14-15 — ____________________ sent for food.

Exodus 10:19 — Locusts swept into the __________ __________.

2 Kings 5:3, 5 — Naaman cured of ____________________.

Exodus 7:4 — Ten plagues were brought upon ____________________.

Acts 20:9 — Young man named ____________________ restored to life.

Acts 14:8-10 — Cripple man at ____________________ made to walk.

Acts 9:40 — ____________________ raised from the dead.

Acts 9:33 — ____________________ cured of palsy.

Matthew 15:32-39 — Feeding the ____________________.

John 2:9 — Water into ____________________.

VIRTUES

```
T H I N K A K I N G C O U L D D O I T B E T T E R G T H
F E L L O W S I H P E U T R I V S T R E N G H T O O U A
C H A R I T E A N U N I S K I T E S A H C H I D L M A N
I N N O S E N C E D A I S Y T L A Y O L A N L A I G H D
N E B E N E V O E L N T E S A H C H A S E I A L R H F Y
C C O R E Y A R P A T E Y T I H R A H C N R I R P G E M
R N B N E M S F A I T K S F A I T N R E A T U R E I L A
E E A I P T O L A R A N S S E S N O C I Y E N A O L L N
D G U N A O E P                         N M D C B T O A
I I N N F L P R                         C G E O E E S T
B L D O O A I A                         O O R N D M H W
E I E S R R H Y                         M D S S I P E O
N D R E G A S A                         P L T I E E T R
C O S N I N W R                         A I O D N R S K
H H T I A F O I                         T N O E S E A D
A K A F V E L N                         I E D R E N H O
N I N E I L L N                         O S I A E S C N
T N D L R O E O                         N S N T R E G O
M D I L C Y F S                         A R G E P O H T
E N N O H A E E                         K N O W L E G C
N E G W E L T N                         I L O Y A L T A
T S N C W T N T                         N H U M I L I U
A T E H Y E E H                         H T G N E R T S
N C R I E D C O                         D N I H T T Y E
O S T P I C O E                         Y O V T E N L U
I T S G C A N P                         T I I U R E Y P
T R N E H R N A                         I T N R N L T S
C E Y G N I I T R N G I D P A T I E N C R A G T I O I E
E N E D Y E D N T E Q E A I T N O I S S A P M O C V N T
F G T E P N V H G U P T S Y L I N G I D H M A L Q E G O
F H I L O R U I I Q I M F T R I N G E R C O F U U N I R
A T N W R R A E G E U L E O A T G I L U D C I M I E D I
D H G O T B T Y N R Y A O T B H U K E C N E I D E B O L
A I I N K L A C R B O K C I U Q C Y D L T R V B T O R L
M N D K Y K E L M E Y F D I L I G E N T C E W D A S E B
```

faith	loyalty
hope	understanding
charity	prayer
virtue	tolerance
knowledge	affection
temperance	forgiveness
patience	innocent
kindness	fellowship
godliness	obedience
humility	considerate
diligence	chaste
strength	benevolent
compassion	caring
dignity	truth

TRANSPORTATION

```
                        R S       A B
                        O E       T L
                        E G       E A
                  L J K S R N T W S C C K Z
                  O E Z R A O H H R K A R I
                  F T L O B I Y E O H R A A
S S R O H P O N Y T E O H T R Z L H E M S C U R T B U G G Y
  A H S K A T E S M O E E T N A N E V O C E H T F O K R A R
    B I C Y C L A L R Z T R U C K L Z T Y K L Y O C A N O E
      A P I G C A M K A I P O N Y A W O C R N A R M Z L Y D
        C O W B L A C K H O R S E P H R L E B D H F O D A R
          B I K E S W H W C O L T O I R A H C S E W E B I L
            S K A T E B O A R D O C E A N L I N E R S C A R
```

1 Nephi 18:1 ______________________________

Ether 2:6 ______________________________

Genesis 6:14 ______________________________

2 Kings 2:11 ______________________________

Revelation 6:2 ______________________________

Revelation 6:5 ______________________________

Matthew 12:40 ______________________________

Proverbs 6:18 ______________________________

Revelation 6:8 ______________________________

Genesis 24:61 ______________________________

Joshua 6:6 ______________________________

BOOK OF MORMON NAMES

```
              R T O N H M U
              O S P E S E K
              S Y P P I N H
              S N R H L E S
              E A O Y B P I
              R G S I A H K
              P O S A T I S
N E P H A I A P G E L S A E T I N A M A L
E D A M M A R O N R H S I L B A T S E S E
P I S E M A G O S K I N K R E S E R P P O
H I T L O O P K U S N E N T Y V H S P E N
Y V A O R N R M S N O M R O M R E A M M A
M A M M O R E O H I R H E Y K U N R O I T
N D A A M N H I N D O S M L G A L E V E R
              S I I M I U O
              A L V H K G M
              L B A S A K O
              E A D N I H M
              V T Y K U S R
              E S T A B I O
              R E D E M K M
```

Mosiah 27:13	This is my church and I will ______________ it.
Helaman 2:5	______________ sought to destroy Helaman.
Alma 45:10	According to the spirit of ______________.
3 Nephi 7:17	Great power given to ______________.
Alma 32:5	Places of worship ______________.
Alma 62:43	Moroni's son ______________.
4 Nephi 47	Brother of Amos ______________.
Mormon 1:5	Mormon's father's name ______________.
Mormon 2:5	Driven out of the land of ______________.
2 Nephi 8:13	And where is the fury of the ______________.

HOW MANY BOOKS OF THE NEW TESTAMENT CAN YOU FIND?

Y	N	O	I	T	A	L	E	V	E	R	E	R	S	J	O	N	E	E
T	H	E	S	S	A	L	O	N	I	E	M	N	S	C	C	E	M	D
H	P	T	I	J	E	S	U	S	S	S	A	M	O	O	I	A	T	U
E	H	E	O	A	T	N	H	N	U	I	A	R	R	I	R	M	A	J
S	I	H	E	M	S	A	A	T	N	S	I	Z	E	K	U	L	C	I
S	N	O	Z	E	I	I	I	O	O	N	E	J	I	U	T	O	R	S
A	I	S	R	S	S	T	L	M	T	P	O	N	L	B	R	N	O	A
L	P	E	A	S	L	A	A	H	S	H	G	U	S	I	A	C	M	I
O	P	A	O	E	S	L	I	R	N	I	K	Z	N	H	O	Y	E	A
M	I	L	O	S	D	A	P	W	A	L	W	T	A	R	X	S	N	H
A	O	J	E	O	N	G	E	L	M	E	H	A	I	O	A	W	S	F
C	A	H	G	S	B	H	T	U	O	M	N	T	S	M	J	J	O	B
A	T	A	C	T	T	E	E	K	R	O	H	H	E	B	R	E	W	S
C	I	W	U	T	Y	C	R	T	J	N	M	U	H	R	U	T	H	K
T	O	N	A	J	O	B	A	P	H	I	L	I	P	P	I	A	N	S
T	N	M	C	O	R	I	N	T	H	E	A	N	E	S	J	O	H	E

1. ____________________ 11. ____________________
2. ____________________ 12. ____________________
3. ____________________ 13. ____________________
4. ____________________ 14. ____________________
5. ____________________ 15. ____________________
6. ____________________ 16. ____________________
7. ____________________ 17. ____________________
8. ____________________ 18. ____________________
9. ____________________ 19. ____________________
10. ____________________ 20. ____________________

FAMOUS NAMES FROM THE SCRIPTURES

A N H M
L N E M Y O A U
R A D H A A R S H S A R
L A Z R P R P R U E A I M H I Y
H U B A E E K J L Y S S T H M S T M H
Y K B R W T E O H T I M S M U R Y H S
E I U A S S H E M N I A A R U Y M
U S U H A N T I P U P T R T T
S R Y M S I R O H I T Y H
E R A T H J E O T H S
U S S O H M H N E
W O I J T A T A W
E B N T A I N I Y N S
R O I S P R M U M D T O S
B C H O U A A S E Y E A T M L
E A P R A H B D H L A B E N E R A
H J E S U C P E O P Y E M T I I L O S
M N Y M E M E H S E L I N L L J B E M
O S Z U U S T H S S H K E A I S A
R M R R O N E O O E U M L O N
O I Y J H M J Z M E O M N
N H H O Y E A S T H A
I T J O S E P H Y
A N T H O N Y
T E R R Y
J I M

2 Chronicles 24:20-21 ______________________

Mark 6:24-25 ______________________

Matthew 27:50 ______________________

Acts 22:20 ______________________

Acts 12:2 ______________________

Mosiah 17:20 ______________________

D&C 135:1 ______________________

____

Revelation 2:13 ______________________

Genesis 4:8 ______________________

DOCTRINAL THEMES

W	I	S	D	U	M	M	A	U	T	H	O	R	E	T	Y
R	E	P	E	N	O	T	R	E	A	S	U	R	Y	M	L
T	R	I	A	D	F	O	R	R	E	T	H	G	U	A	D
T	R	E	S	S	P	A	S	M	A	L	E	L	O	W	H
S	M	I	T	Y	N	O	I	T	N	E	T	N	O	C	O
O	W	S	E	P	R	S	Y	L	A	I	N	T	E	D	N
Z	S	E	T	A	E	B	C	A	T	G	A	B	L	M	E
Y	B	R	U	R	A	C	Y	U	B	V	D	B	I	W	S
A	D	U	E	W	H	A	D	T	A	D	N	S	B	Y	D
D	E	S	X	Y	E	E	L	H	T	N	E	P	E	R	E
V	M	A	P	T	A	M	Y	O	U	R	C	R	R	U	L
E	R	E	A	Z	E	S	E	R	Y	E	S	A	T	N	L
N	O	R	C	G	O	G	H	I	J	M	E	K	Y	N	I
T	F	T	Y	F	Y	A	N	T	R	O	D	A	O	E	F
U	E	B	K	P	I	Y	O	Y	O	K	A	M	U	R	L
R	D	M	T	Q	U	I	T	E	P	O	L	E	R	S	U
E	T	N	E	M	H	S	I	N	O	T	S	A	S	I	F

1 Nephi 8:33	And great was the multitude	
Ether 5:6	For ye shall know that I have authority	
2 Nephi 3:4	And I am a descendant	
Mormon 2:8	They did not ________	
2 Nephi 12:6	And hearken unto ________	
Helaman 13:19	That they shall hide up their ________	
Alma 2:1	There began to be a ________ ________	
3 Nephi 15:5	The law in me is ________	
Alma 62:4	Standard of ________	
2 Nephi 3:10	Out of the land of ________	
Ether 8:11	The ________ of Jared	
3 Nephi 10:2	For so great was the ________	
Alma 32:12	That ye may learn ________	
Helaman 3:29	Gulf of ________	
3 Nephi 8:17	The whole earth became ________	

GOSPEL TERMS

```
                  A G F Y T N E M W O D N E
                D T N A T E L S E G U F E R N
              M N I I I G N I R E T S I N I M E
            N E R O T T N O I T A D N U O F N I M
          G M T S H S H N N D U R H E R E R U D N E
        I E S W I N A F A E S O E L A I R T E L E C N
      T N E B N O M F U A E M R M O T N E M A M R I F O
    S O R L G T W R K L I T I E E I N Y H N L I P S I D T
  A T R N A U K L O S R W T S A N F N O R T I A N A O L N T
F A E Y P I B A W N E H A N D T T O S E I M I R I M G E S I A
W T O L T R I E O T D N I M U   N A T N D T E T I T M U P E K
O E L A E T W T S N C O I P       E R A O T A N E E S H F I T
R R A G S S A Y U E N N T           M T E I I S N R S E N E R
S A N E T E M O R I I A               D S O T O N R I G L A R
T P L U I R F E M S N                   N I T A O E D P P E W
H E R F M R T O T I                       A N W N O P E S O C
T R E E O E D E D                           M I M I R S Y N T
R P T R N T R R                               M M P D A I S A
U W E O Y B O                                   O D F R E D M
T H I T H E                                       C A T O N Y
```

refuge
endure
fasting
endowment
terrestrial
testimony
worship
telestial
inheritance
celestial
prepare
tithing
firmament

ordinations
mysteries
dominion
administer
atonement
commandments
ministering
kingdom
foundation
eternal
faithful
dispensation

PSALM 23

D	A	Y	S	R	E	M	S	S	E	M	D	O	O	G	E	S	E
S	Y	A	D	H	E	R	C	P	M	U	K	Y	R	N	T	S	N
Y	E	R	Y	R	U	O	R	A	R	V	A	E	E	S	E	E	E
L	S	K	F	N	M	E	L	E	A	D	E	T	H	D	F	N	M
T	U	Y	N	F	S	E	S	L	D	N	H	A	T	W	I	S	Y
S	O	E	O	E	A	T	L	R	P	Y	D	V	E	E	L	U	E
E	H	R	N	D	O	T	E	A	E	O	L	E	D	L	O	O	S
R	T	C	E	R	H	H	S	V	W	T	I	V	A	L	V	E	S
A	E	T	E	Y	P	T	I	E	M	K	A	I	E	T	E	T	E
P	T	T	A	E	U	L	V	E	T	L	Y	W	L	A	H	H	I
E	H	D	H	R	O	D	R	L	L	N	D	V	L	I	E	G	M
R	A	S	E	F	B	C	A	E	C	E	I	D	R	O	L	I	E
P	M	S	C	T	Y	W	Y	F	A	H	T	O	N	N	U	R	N
W	A	T	E	S	R	B	A	T	H	T	E	N	N	U	R	I	E
S	S	E	N	D	O	O	G	L	A	W	O	D	H	A	S	G	T

1. The Lord is my ________________; I shall not want.

2. He maketh me to lie down in ________ ________: he ________________ me beside the still ________________.

3. He ________________ my soul: he ________________ me in the paths of ________________ for his name's sake.

4. Yea, though I walk through the ________________ of the ________________ of ________________, I will fear no ________: for thou art with me; thy ________ and thy ________________ they ________________ me.

5. Thou ________________ a table before me in the ________________ of mine ________________: thou ________________ my head with oil; my cup________________over.

6. Surely ________________ and ________________ shall follow me all the ________ of my ________: and I will ________________ in the ________________ of the ________________ for ever.

MORE
BOOK OF MORMON NAMES AND PHRASES

```
X
B Y                         I N
A E H                     N A R C
N L Z I                 T I S O Y K
T O E M R             E D R N L O D
I M D P T O         R A E F L R E
P Z E H D R K   T G T O A I Z
A D K A H Y A T A E U H H L
R E I R U A E D R N T U K
A D A A H R I P I E R O
A N A P S A R K R T R
H U L I N E R U E I I R
C O M T T Y D O H D W O S
H F O N W N C O M F E K N T
O N I A E H R Y L U G Z I S Y
R O J A V S R I O H C E D A H M
U C N T R U D N E L A R O M U C A
S G A D I A N S M O I T I D A R T X
```

Helaman 7:25	Secret band established by	______________________
Mormon 8:2	Great and tremendous battle at	______________________
Alma 56:34	Strongest Lamanite army stationed at	______________________
Alma 38:2	For blessed is he that	______________________
1 Nephi 14:2	Shall no more be	______________________
Alma 24:7	And to convince us of the	______________________
Alma 30:12	Anti-Christ	______________________
Mormon 7:7	Groups of singers	______________________
1 Nephi 1:4	King of Judah	______________________
Ether 4:5	Wherefore I have sealed up the	______________________

BOOK OF MORMON CITIES

S	A	L	T	L	A	K	E	C	I	T	Y	C	O	L	U	M	B	U	S	E	R	I	E	C	P
L	O	G	A	N	S	P	O	K	A	N	E	M	A	D	I	S	O	N	E	V	A	D	A	I	R
D	E	N	V	E	R	N	E	W	O	R	L	E	A	N	S	H	E	R	M	A	N	E	O	N	E
S	A	R	A	T	O	G	A	S	J	E	N	N	I	N	G	S	Z	M	A	R	Y	Z	M	C	S
A	R	T	I	R	E	I	O	E	A	M	U	C	O	M	O	R	S	E	O	O	Z	O	O	I	T
C	N	E	V	A	D	A	R	G	R	E	E	N	B	A	Y	A	N	C	I	L	L	Z	R	N	O
R	O	A	Z	I	T	S	Y	O	N	E	M	U	K	H	S	I	K	L	O	I	I	C	G	N	N
A	N	N	A	L	A	K	E	S	M	I	A	M	I	Z	I	O	N	U	H	G	X	H	A	A	H
M	I	C	K	L	A	G	L	I	G	A	D	I	O	M	N	A	H	K	I	H	Y	I	S	T	U
E	J	U	E	A	L	D	O	M	E	L	A	S	U	R	E	J	F	E	T	T	F	C	H	I	D
N	A	M	Y	L	B	A	I	L									A	L	O	G	N	A	E	D	S
T	C	K	O	M	E	G	T	E									I	U	X	Y	H	G	B	E	O
O	O	X	Z	E	R	A	R	H									T	M	R	I	T	O	R	T	N
A	B	H	E	H	T	T	E	I									N	Y	N	N	R	X	O	R	A
T	K	O	A	A	H	O	Z	N									A	O	S	E	O	N	O	O	M
L	L	U	R	R	T	R	A	E									M	X	T	M	P	O	K	I	A
A	U	S	A	A	A	S	O	P	E	I	P	M	A	G	L	M	Y	R	A	U	E	I	E	T	R
N	F	T	M	Z	G	P	B	H	O	Z	O	A	R	L	A	G	R	I	O	C	V	T	L	N	I
T	I	O	I	X	U	R	I	I	Z	N	R	F	E	A	M	F	A	N	B	L	E	A	K	O	L
A	T	N	N	J	B	A	I	T	I	O	J	O	T	D	A	L	A	D	X	O	R	L	R	R	L
N	N	A	O	I	O	M	Y	H	N	X	G	Q	M	E	N	I	O	L	I	T	H	O	E	F	O
D	U	Z	R	R	C	R	A	Y	L	A	N	N	E	S	D	N	G	X	Q	A	S	S	T	O	G
A	O	T	O	H	A	H	I	N	O	R	O	M	L	A	J	T	R	O	Y	Z	N	E	O	L	A
I	B	Z	M	I	J	M	E	M	P	H	I	S	G	O	S	H	S	O	J	I	M	D	O	K	N
L	O	N	G	V	I	E	W	D	E	N	V	E	R	N	A	S	H	V	I	L	L	E	I	Y	S

(BOOK OF MORMON CITIES)

Alma 52:17 (2)

____

____

Mosiah 7:21 (2)

____

____

Alma 8:13

____

Alma 8:6

____

Mormon 2:4

____

Mormon 4:20

____

Alma 56:14 (4)

____

____

____

____

Mormon 4:3 (2)

____

____

3 Nephi 9:3-10 (16)

____

____

____

____

____

____

____

____

____

____

____

____

____

____

____

____

DO YOU KNOW THE LATTER-DAY PROPHETS?
FIND ALL 15 OF THEM.

H	B	N	J	O	S	E	P	H	S	M	I	T	H	J	R	J	Q	G	H	Z
W	G	H	O	E	Z	R	A	T	A	F	T	B	E	N	S	O	N	Z	E	W
H	V	M	H	S	P	E	N	C	E	R	W	K	I	M	B	A	L	L	W	G
L	G	J	N	D	L	O	R	E	N	Z	O	S	N	O	W	M	N	H	I	E
F	T	E	T	L	Y	E	I	X	O	H	J	L	R	V	B	S	F	W	L	O
H	O	W	A	R	D	W	H	U	N	T	E	R	D	L	H	O	Y	V	F	R
E	A	R	Y	X	J	Y	E	L	K	C	N	I	H	B	N	O	D	R	O	G
B	S	W	L	I	K	H	Q	J	Q	Q	N	V	C	V	L	O	G	P	R	E
E	L	R	O	H	J	U	P	M	Y	M	R	K	H	P	G	E	L	F	D	A
R	T	B	R	I	G	H	A	M	Y	O	U	N	G	D	R	Y	E	H	W	L
J	O	S	E	P	H	F	I	E	L	D	I	N	G	S	M	I	T	H	O	B
G	O	M	I	G	G	R	T	D	H	Q	T	R	I	K	V	N	T	T	O	E
R	E	S	O	P	J	I	M	E	A	N	T	Y	B	F	M	R	I	O	D	R
A	J	N	E	X	Q	O	U	T	M	J	T	V	M	S	R	E	I	D	R	T
N	G	R	Q	P	S	W	O	N	T	A	T	R	G	R	R	L	T	E	U	S
T	I	K	Q	N	H	K	V	K	I	B	C	I	T	J	H	I	C	Q	F	M
H	G	Y	L	V	A	F	N	G	D	M	K	D	J	G	W	V	X	R	F	I
R	D	F	O	S	B	O	S	O	E	X	N	A	T	H	D	J	M	E	W	T
I	F	D	A	V	I	D	O	M	C	K	A	Y	N	J	N	Z	D	U	O	H
G	P	C	Y	J	L	B	R	P	I	W	U	S	A	I	L	Y	Z	Q	D	J
Q	F	C	L	R	Q	I	Q	Q	H	T	B	N	Y	O	V	T	T	W	S	M
P	N	S	C	M	D	L	X	J	S	D	H	N	O	F	V	D	Q	P	X	C

1. ______________________
2. ______________________
3. ______________________
4. ______________________
5. ______________________
6. ______________________
7. ______________________
8. ______________________
9. ______________________
10. ______________________
11. ______________________
12. ______________________
13. ______________________
14. ______________________
15. ______________________

SCRIPTURE GEMS

```
D O C A T D U N T A S Z H E O W F C R P H T E S
O T G A O R E I D N A E C Y O R O I E A R Y I Y
C E R C T I L M A R T N T R P N D E R S T N P R
M T T S D I I M A O A N K I O O C I K M N I C C
S R N E N N K H M T R M E I R N C A N M A O N O
I I B I I O E P N E A G T M A C Z R E A N M C S
  O S S R M I E R N G A A R A A O D I S T D E
    T W L E P T S I N A B N R M U P E E N I
      L H E T H C I V M T A I T R C Y A T
        R T I S D U E I H A I Z R I E H
          P N R I M R E L L R A E N F
            O E E N M T I E T T I D
              R I L I M S I G R S
                A D I M O N T E
                  S E N D C I
                    S B O A
                      D O
```

Moses 1:6	And thou art in the ____________________
Abraham 4:31	They shall be very ____________________
Moses 2:6	Let there be a ____________________
Moses 7:36	And among all the ____________________
D&C 132:3	To receive and obey the ____________________
D&C 125:3	And let the name of ____________________
D&C 68:1	Was called by his ____________________
JS—H 2:60	Every ____________________ that could . . .
11th Art. of Faith	We claim the ____________________
D&C 83:6	Shall be kept by the ____________________
Moses 6:46	For a book of ____________________
D&C 124:98	From those who would ____________________
Abraham 4:25	And the Gods ____________________ the earth.
D&C 50:8	But the ____________________ shall be detected.
D&C 10:62	True points of my ____________________
D&C 18:6	Stirred up unto ____________________

A POTPOURRI OF SCRIPTURE TERMS

C	E	N	T	U	R	Y	O	N	F	R	A	N	K	I	N	S	E	N	C	E	M	U	R
O	E	G	A	T	T	O	P	H	O	A	R	A	H	P	H	T	O	L	C	K	C	A	S
N	T	O	G	U	I	T	I	M	R	B	F	H	C	Y	M	B	I	U	Y	G	O	M	A
V	C	N	A	N	M	G	O	M	G	R	S	C	F	C	H	C	N	P	M	A	N	U	C
E	A	Y	L	L	B	R	A	L	A	N	O	Y	E	L	Y	L	T	O	B	L	V	N	K
R	T	C	B	E	R	C	A	N	N	N	N	N	C	M	E	S	M	T	A	B	E	A	K
T	S	H	A	A	E	B	K	E	S	O	T	O	B	A	O	T	E	T	L	A	R	B	L
I	O	H	N	D	L	I	C	V	I	U	N	A	V	I	E	A	N	E	S	N	S	L	O
O	R	A	O	A	N	N	E	S	R	V	L	E	N	R	P	T	T	G	Y	M	I	A	T
N	G	N	M	C	I	R	R	I	E	E	N	T	B	O	U	C	N	E	D	U	O	G	H
M	I	A	E	K	S	E	O	R	S	E	M	M	T	N	A	E	W	A	L				
A	C	N	N	I	V	N	T	Y	D	E	I	T	L	E	V						E	P	O
E	S	A	O	N	W	I	K	R	N	T	A						H	S	P	N	O	R	I
E	R	N	O	N	O	P	E						E	T	C	U	A	R	C	I	E	T	N
F	S	C	S						A	C	K	N	L	I	T	C	E	Y	S	M	R	R	T
					T	C	E	P	E	X	C	A	K	M	K	P	C	E	N	Y	E	P	M
E	R	H	A	R	H	L	O	N	D	Y	P	O	E	B	A	L	N	N	H	M	D	N	E
L	E	O	Y	S	K	S	T	E	C	O	R	O	N	R	O	P	A	I	A	A	E	O	N
K	M	A	A	N	T	U	P	L	S	S	R	F	A	P	G	H	O	S	R	C	R	I	S
E	N	R	H	E	R	O	O	I	A	G	E	D	H	N	T	N	P	R	K	E	A	T	T
N	O	A	L	I	L	P	T	B	E	J	O	L	O	S	Y	K	B	E	C	D	P	R	A
K	N	H	O	C	E	L	G	N	W	N	T	S	T	Y	W	S	L	V	A	O	E	E	C
O	A	P	Y	D	E	R	S	A	Y	L	I	Y	S	S	T	N	A	N	M	E	R	V	E
R	P	C	I	S	O	T	J	H	B	O	W	N	G	I	O	K	Y	O	H	N	P	N	T
S	N	A	L	I	B	N	H	A	P	H	A	R	A	H	O	P	E	C	A	I	I	O	R
E	S	M	A	H	M	A	C	K	H	A	R	V	R	Y	E	P	A	W	M	A	E	C	E

(A POTPOURRI OF SCRIPTURE TERMS)

Genesis 37:34	A type of clothing	______
Psalms 150:4-5	Instruments (3)	______ ______ ______
D&C 1:14	Twelve	______
Exodus 30:34	Sweet spices (3)	______ ______ ______
D&C 123:5	Educational volumes	______
Genesis 41:25	Ruler of Egypt	______
Exodus 12:15	Without rising agent	______
D&C 113:10	Pieces	______
Matthew 26:6-7	Oily fragrant substance	______
Genesis 25:33-34	Birthright sold for	______
D&C 84:72	Venom	______
Matthew 8:5	Roman officer	______
D&C 45:61	To be made ready	______
Acts 16:9	A Greek territory	______
Acts 15:3	A changing	______
Abraham 1:6	Evil gods (5)	______ ______ ______ ______ ______

PRIESTHOOD POSITIONS

```
                    A
                  A B H
                R L I P T
              O M G H R E N
            N H H Y E O M Y E
          C O P T R S P P M T D
        I M R S U U E H L Y P N I
      N A I F T L A R E E M A S E S
    O P E N P D O O H T S E I R P V E
  R Y S T I C K I S   R E D L E A V E R
A A T Y R T N E T       Y R E V E R N S P
A N C H C O R S D           A L E P S O G T A
  B O S N O C A E D       A W I L O P A M U
    R I S E N T Z I P   P R O R A A Y R T
      A S G A D I A R O M E K A T S I H
        N S N E H Y S P A H L R O S O
          C I I C T I M E C I V R R
            H M L O V E M A R Y I
              E E A T Y R E M T
                M O E C I T Y
                  T H H O E
                    A L T
                      A
```

Prophet	Aaronic
Seer	Priest
Revelator	Teacher
Melchizedek	Deacon
Priesthood	Stake
Patriarch	Authority
Truth	Gospel
Apostle	Scripture
High Priest	Healing
Seventy	Temples
Elder	President
Mission	Ward
Love	Branch

MORE BOOK OF MORMON TERMS

```
        Y N T I S T X E
      G O L A F E R Y O M
    G L O A T S C O T S L I
  Y B E Y E R C R A F T Y M Y
N I A T N U O F E L R T V P O W
M H E M O C R E A T P H N I E U O L
S A M S O S N S F C T S E D R A M I
P A N I A N T I W O M E M I F N E B
U N D E R O L O G M B W E U E O N E
T R I P L I T A X B T Y C S C M E R
A B K R F T H E I I P X N N T R P T
T L C E Y A W T C N I T E O I O I Y
I C A D U T Z W X A F X M I O M H C
  O L P H U L G H T T G M S N X I
    B Z O P J O Y I S K O N S S
      N A S A H N O T Z C A O
        O I K C E N K E Y M
          D T R O S T L N
```

3 Nephi 18:34	No ______________________ among you.
Helaman 15:5	And they do walk ______________ before God.
Alma 63:5	Builder of ships ______________________
Mosiah 18:5	Now there was in Mormon a ______________
Alma 21:11	The name of a village ______________________
Enos 27	Prepared for you in the ______________________
Mormon 8:12	Because of the ______________ which are in it.
2 Nephi 26:22	These will open safes __________ __________
Alma 38:5	Alma's son ______________________
Alma 56:20	This comes before graduation ______________
3 Nephi 2:15	Their ______________ was taken from them.
3 Nephi 3:8	Until ye shall become ______________________
Alma 5:58	Book of ______________________
3 Nephi 12:36	Colors (2) __________ __________

PEOPLE, PLACES AND THINGS

```
G Z A R A I S A I A O D R E Z A P O
I A L M E H A R A Z A A E A A L E P
D T I S E A C I R P T N R S R E N E
D B F K A I L M E T N A E N E O I R
I O L O T A M R U I H F O R S R O T
A N E O M S D Z N H M E B I B L E I
N E S B O I M E L A S U R E J Z A T
H S H M T D S D L S H P O N R A M I
I L I I M U N E S N I T N O D P I O
S T O P B E H K N A O I M Y L O N N
H N Y O A N M I L I M N A H O T A S
U T O A L P E A R L N I N E G O D E
N L Y E A N O H A I L E A H O T I O
B E Z A R A H E M L O L A O S I R P
```

1 Nephi 7:7	Where?	________________
1 Nephi 5:12	King	________________
Mosiah 23:20	City	________________
Alma 11:5	Gold (4)	______ ______ ______ ______
Alma 11:6	Silver (4)	______ ______ ______ ______
Alma 10:13	Into	________________
3 Nephi 27:32	Son of	________________
3 Nephi 16:17	Prophet	________________
Alma 22:27	Land of	________________
Mormon 6:15	Body components (3)	______ ______ ______
Alma 37:38	Compass	________________
Alma 10:2	Interpreted	________________
3 Nephi 3:9	Governor	________________
Ether 2:3	Honey bee	________________

DOCTRINES FROM THE DOCTRINE AND COVENANTS

N I V I G S K N A H T H Y Z
G Z I T N E I D E P X E A C
M Z I A N S A I R A H C A Z
A D M C D Z N E D T S P M A
W N G E M H E A X A R T E I
O N P T U A M P M I W T L Y
F I I E I A T H E O B E I L
T F T P H C A R E U A T E R
Z A Y I E A S I B I D R I N
L I F T D L D D L A E O N P
P U M F I A U N R E E D R I
B M I T N B O W A R S O U T
W I U N I O G M I E W P D M
R T G O N P A T R T E W A R
R T A A N D O D M I T S T E
E B M S I Z A C H A R I S A
V I G N I V I G S K N A H T
R E E D E M E D E X P E D I

D&C 127:2 — To glory in ____________________

D&C 43:30 — The great ____________________ shall come.

D&C 70:11 — Appointed in a ____________________

D&C 24:3 — ____________________ thine office.

D&C 116 — Where Adam dwelt ____________________

D&C 27:7 — Father of John ____________________

D&C 88:137 — November holiday ____________________

D&C 109:77 — Hear us in these our ____________________

D&C 42:57 — And it is ____________________

D&C 136:18 — Zion shall be ____________________

D&C 98:3 — With an ____________________ covenant.

D&C 130:21 — Upon which it is ____________________

A FEW THINGS MISSIONARIES SHOULD HAVE

M A M A S A N D D A D D Y S I S
I G E M S A E C N A R U D N E E I A
L E S B A A L Y G I R L E S T R M L P N
K T Y U E I L T A N P H S P A U H O K P W D
C T D T B A L A G E R O I A X T T C N N L A G W
O E N I R S U O C A A R R M I P I O O E E E T R H I
O L A U M U I T V Y Y B E I E I A P W A Y E S E O I C C
K S C S Z U C S I E E Y C A L R F T L Y T N P T R C S E T H
I A E U S K T F R T D Z I C F A E S I S I A A M E H Y E
E S E I S E U A Z U Y S B O D L R E U A D M E R E S
S U C S N L D P T S O H G Y L O H T R S P L I C
P A A C F I U S H O E S S O C K S U F S O A
R G E E O O P S N O I N A P M O C N I N
A E M A S T E R C A R D F R I E N D

Unscramble the words and locate them in the puzzle block.

deegklnow
raserlerf
siered
reciptsrus
tafih
cradenuen
noisytemt
rreayp
bccesyli
glhshotoy
ebceinssstu
deepsnak
acimnnoops
spam
ynome
dusty

HOW GOOD ARE YOU?

Try finding the words in this puzzle without turning the book around.

```
T W A R N O I T A C I F I T S U J G A U T H O R I T Y E N
O M I R A C L E R E D R O D E T I N U T K M L Y U T C E L
L B I N T E L L I G E N C E T H R I C E D E A H I N V R O
  U I M S E Y A R T H E T O N D P D E W O R W C E A E P
    A B M K A A B E S R E V E R E N C E M C G G E V R
      P L U C C I R I I H K M I R A N S I Y I H I A
        N E H R H A A T R J A G S T A U N L V L Y
          O S T L O Y H U H R H O S T N I F E E
            I S D Y L D A O C T N R N D O D R
              S H N G I Y M A H A E E A N O
                R E A O N F S A G D P Y I
                  E P M L E I N E N E S
                    M E I D S D S U R
                      M R R E S E E
                        I D U N M
                          T A M
                            I
```

dominion
personages
diligence
reverence
sacrament
Urim and Thummim
intelligence
Abraham
understanding
united order
lawgiver
judge

justification
trials
teach
Bible
city
warn
gird
holiness
immersion
authority
prayer
grace
repentance

deliver
Sunday
golden
thrice
miracle
heaven
mercy
Christ
edify
Paul
heirs
right hand

VIRTUES AND BLESSINGS

O C O N T E N T M E N T C O M
S K N O W L E E G T E M P E R A N S E G Y
T N Y K S S E N D N I K Y L R E H T O R B
D H O H T N K N P D C I E V R E S S D H E K H
I G N U H I O E U O T H R P E R E L O C Y O T
L U O M O W R R M N F U W E L C I N N L N P Y
I O I I L S A A E I R Y M Q F N N A Y E E R D
G H S L E N N M H E I X E U E F R E S W G K N
E T S I C D T A B C E T V S B E U T G H D O I
N N A E T I F I M N N E R T V M Y S T I E R M
S A P T M E D U E G O L O P
E E M M O I S T S I N W I N
T L O Y R T S R O E E V O L D
C C O A E I T N A N L
H P N V S S K
S E N S S
F V N E E
A I E N N
I G H G I
S R H N L
T H O U I D O
N Y P F O L O E N
E M E R G E L G Y M E
R K L Y T I L I M U H O I
A H T I A F A I W K N O W H R
P T R A E H E C N A R E P M E T F

(VIRTUES AND BLESSINGS)

WE MUST HAVE:

D&C 4:6 (11) ______________, ______________, ______________,

______________, ______________, ______________, ______________,

______________, ______________, ______________, ______________

D&C 84:41 ____

D&C 64:2; 3 Nephi 17:7 ______________________________

WE MUST ALSO HAVE:

endurance ● longsuffering ● love ● perseverance ● honesty ● hope

clean thoughts ● willingness to serve ● commitment

AND WE ARE INDEED BLESSED IF WE HAVE:

loving ____________, caring ____________, a happy ____________,

a sincere ________________, a desire to ________________.

IF WE POSSESS ALL OF THE ABOVE, WE WILL HAVE:

peace of __________________ and __________________.

Z WHAT YOU CAN DO WITH Z'S

E	Z	U	L	U	Z	O	N	E	Z	O	O	T	O	Z	Z	U	Z
Z	I	Z	L	E	B	A	B	B	U	R	E	Z	Z	A	E	Z	O
I	N	H	U	Z	Z	A	C	C	H	A	E	U	S	P	N	Z	W
L	C	A	N	B	E	Z	F	Z	Z	L	M	Z	O	H	I	A	I
C	Z	R	N	I	B	R	O	F	O	E	A	A	A	Z	T	R	E
H	E	O	U	Z	R	R	U	T	I	R	D	N	R	M	H	E	Z
Z	S	P	L	E	A	E	E	B	A	Z	M	E	A	O	U	P	O
I	T	P	U	M	Z	S	Z	H	B	E	Z	R	K	E	Z	H	O
G	Z	I	B	P	I	Z	E	Z	H	A	O	A	P	I	Z	A	I
Z	G	Z	E	R	A	M	E	A	I	Z	B	Z	N	Z	A	T	D
A	A	E	Z	E	L	E	R	Z	E	Z	E	E	E	O	Z	H	T
G	L	U	Z	A	Z	E	N	I	F	F	O	N	L	O	A	Z	M
U	K	S	Z	R	Z	O	D	I	A	C	A	O	O	E	R	H	O
Z	I	P	O	Z	O	M	B	I	E	N	E	C	M	S	Z	E	O
Z	Z	M	H	A	I	N	A	H	P	E	Z	K	Z	A	P	A	Z

(Z WHAT YOU CAN DO WITH Z'S)

1 Kings 17:9	City where Elijah dwelt	________________
Alma 10:31	A lawyer	________________
Exodus 2:21	Wife of Moses	________________
Mosiah 7:9	Grandfather of Limhi	________________
Ezra 2:2	Also known as Sheshbazzer	________________
Alma 16:5	Chief captain	________________
Luke 6:14-15	Simon and others called	________________
Mosiah 11:8	Precious metal	________________
2 Kings 25:18	Second Priest	________________
3 Nephi 10:16	Two prophets	________ ________
Joshua 15:31, 34, 37	Cities (3)	______ ______ ______
Alma 43:5	Leader of Zoramites	________________
Genesis 30:20	Son of Jacob and Leah	________________
Alma 2:22	A spy	________________
Luke 19:2-5	Climbed a tree to see Jesus	________________
3 Nephi 8:8	City	________________
Jeremiah 49:34	King of Judah	________________
1 Nephi 4:35	Servant of Laban	________________
Ether 12:30	Mountain	________________

NEW TESTAMENT TEACHINGS

C	H	U	R	N	E	M	D	N	A	B	S	U	H	E
L	O	R	D	E	A	C	O	N	S	U	R	S	E	E
W	I	C	K	E	D	D	W	E	F	E	P	A	L	R
H	E	R	G	J	M	Q	E	F	D	E	O	L	P	M
N	W	E	T	Y	O	F	E	E	D	D	H	V	N	R
O	F	T	E	M	N	R	M	E	F	S	S	A	S	A
I	E	E	V	K	I	P	I	D	A	S	I	T	N	W
T	S	E	D	U	T	I	T	A	E	B	B	I	A	E
A	C	M	L	I	I	F	I	S	H	E	S	O	I	K
T	H	E	O	S	O	M	U	N	T	R	Y	N	T	U
P	E	N	S	R	N	E	F	B	I	U	X	M	A	L
M	W	A	G	E	M	O	D	N	A	A	H	P	L	A
E	L	O	M	O	D	F	E	E	F	E	E	B	A	L
T	O	I	R	A	C	S	I	S	A	D	U	J	G	M
I	D	A	U	G	H	T	E	R	D	E	E	E	F	S
N	O	T	N	O	I	T	C	E	R	R	U	S	E	R

(NEW TESTAMENT TEACHINGS)

Luke 21:28	Your ________________ draweth nigh.
Revelation 1:11	I am ________ ________ ________.
Ephesians 6:4	Bring them up in nurture and ________________.
John 21:16	________________________ my sheep.
Matthew 6:4	That thine ______________ may be in secret.
Titus 1:7	For a ______________ must be blameless.
1 Peter 3:11	Let him ______________________ evil.
John 21:15	________________________ my lambs.
Matthew 5:3-11	These are called the ________________.
Acts 27:7	We sailed under ____________________.
2 Corinthians 5:7	For we walk by ______________, not by sight.
Mark 5:34	______________ thy faith hath made thee whole.
Hebrews 2:3	If we neglect so great ________________.
Acts 23:11	So must thou bear witness also at ____________.
John 6:71	He spake of __________ ____________.
1 Timothy 3:12	Let the __________ be the husbands of one wife.
Galatians 3:1	O foolish ______________________.
Luke 20:9	And let it forth to ____________________.
Matthew 19:14	______________________ little children.
John 21:10	Bring of the ______________________.
Revelation 3:16	So then because thou art ________________.
John 11:25	I am the ________________________.
Matthew 6:13	Not into ________________________.
2 Thessalonians 2:8	And then shall that ______________ be revealed.
John 21:17	Jesus said unto him, ____________ my sheep.

FIND 26 KINGS IN THE BOOK OF MORMON

A	L	M	A	C	E	T	H	E	R	A	A	E	I	O	U	Y
L	U	E	N	O	B	K	A	V	Z	M	L	H	N	L	B	E
M	A	N	O	H	E	A	R	T	H	A	E	R	T	H	O	M
C	N	N	R	O	N	I	S	H	U	L	E	M	O	Q	C	O
G	O	V	W	R	J	Z	N	Y	I	I	K	W	U	S	A	R
U	A	R	E	A	A	A	X	H	N	C	I	O	I	V	J	M
L	H	S	I	K	M	Y	P	E	L	K	B	W	G	K	Y	O
R	I	K	H	A	I	E	Z	E	N	I	F	F	N	E	Z	N
H	M	M	L	U	N	W	K	L	L	A	C	Z	O	T	D	C
E	S	U	H	I	F	T	E	H	A	H	J	I	E	H	I	H
T	L	A	T	I	F	V	U	A	E	M	F	E	L	E	G	R
H	R	N	N	N	O	R	O	M	M	A	O	A	S	M	M	I
T	A	E	U	L	A	T	M	M	D	O	R	N	I	U	A	S
E	Z	N	I	F	F	I	I	O	N	E	Z	T	I	T	S	T
N	E	P	H	I	K	P	R	R	L	A	E	U	H	C	H	L
F	O	R	G	I	V	E	C	O	M	A	H	M	R	O	E	O
O	H	L	O	V	E	S	T	M	C	B	P	O	E	L	M	R
C	H	E	R	I	S	N	O	R	A	A	M	O	P	R	T	D
M	O	M	T	R	A	B	I	N	I	D	I	E	H	E	O	S

Mosiah 11:27	______________	Omni 24	______________
Mosiah 19:29	______________	Alma 17:21	______________
Mormon 2:9	______________	Ether 10:32	______________
Alma 2:9	______________	Alma 47:35	______________
Alma 52:3	______________	Alma 24:3	______________
Ether 10:32	______________	Ether 7:15	______________
Ether 7:20	______________	Ether 9:21	______________
Ether 9:21	______________	Ether 12:1	______________
Ether 11:11	______________	Ether 10:30	______________
Ether 9:26	______________	3 Nephi 7:9-10	______________
Ether 7:3	______________	Ether 10:13	______________
Ether 10:17	______________	Ether 10:18	______________
Mosiah 7:21	______________	Mosiah 7:21	______________

PLACES AND THINGS FROM THE BOOK OF MORMON

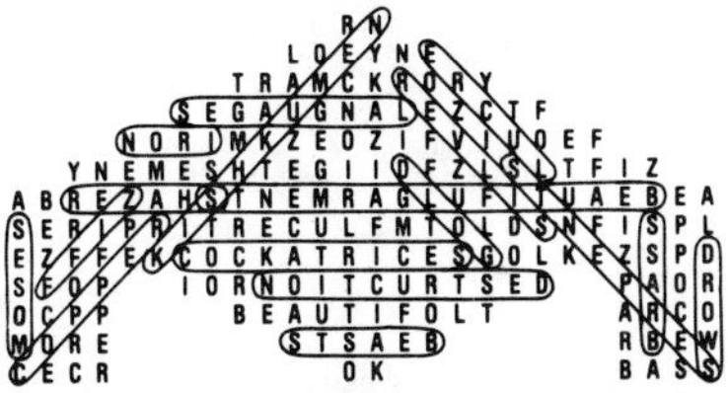

Campsite	SHAZER	1 Nephi 16:13
Money	LUCRE	Mosiah 29:40
Den	COCKATRICES	2 Nephi 21:8
Weapon	SWORD	Alma 2:1
Hunt	BEASTS	Enos 3
Law	MOSES	Jarom 11
Confounded	LANGUAGE	Omni 22
Witnessed	DESTRUCTION	Words of Mormon 1
Murderer	KISHKUMEN	Helaman 1:9
Clothing	BEAUTIFUL GARMENTS	Moroni 10:31
Poisonous	SERPENTS	Ether 10:19
Metals (6)	GOLD	Mosiah 11:3
	SILVER	
	ZIFF	
	COPPER	
	BRASS	
	IRON	

11

JESUS WAS:

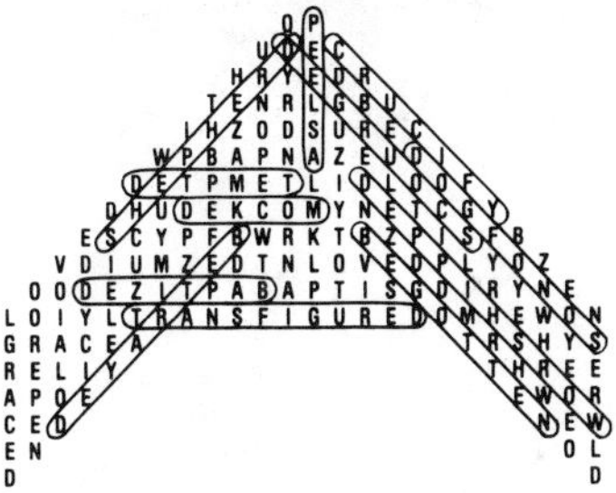

Luke 4:2, 4; 12	TEMPTED
John 19:1	SCOURGED
Mark 4:38	ASLEEP
Matthew 3:13	BAPTIZED
Matthew 17:2	TRANSFIGURED
Matthew 26:24	BETRAYED
John 10:11	SHEPHERD
John 3:18	BEGOTTEN
Mark 15:13	CRUCIFIED
John 9:38	WORSHIPPED
Mark 15:20	MOCKED
Mark 15:39	SON OF GOD

12

LAND AND WATER

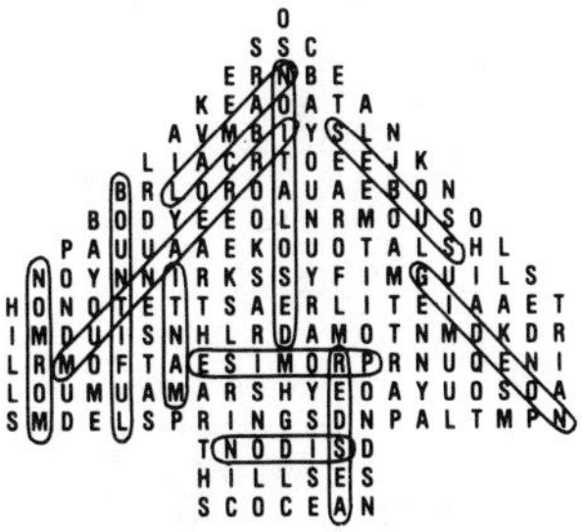

Water	SEBUS	Alma 17:26
Water	IRREANTUM	1 Nephi 17:5
Land	BOUNTIFUL	1 Nephi 17:5
Water	RED SEA	1 Nephi 17:26
Water	SIDON	Alma 3:3
Water	MORMON	Mosiah 18:8
Land	PROMISE	1 Nephi 2:20
Land	GIDEON	Alma 6:8
Land	JERUSALEM	1 Nephi 17:20
Land	MANTI	Alma 43:42
Land	DESOLATION	Alma 22:30
River	LAMAN	1 Nephi 2:8

13

"ITES" OF THE BOOK OF MORMON

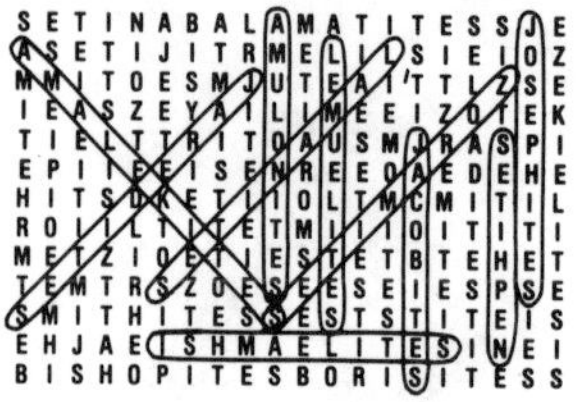

Jacob 1:13 (7)	LAMANITES
	NEPHITES
	JACOBITES
	JOSEPHITES
	ZORAMITES
	LEMUELITES
	ISHMAELITES
Moroni 9:23	JAREDITES
Alma 25:29 (2)	AMALEKITES
	AMULONITES

14

12 DISCIPLES CHOSEN BY JESUS

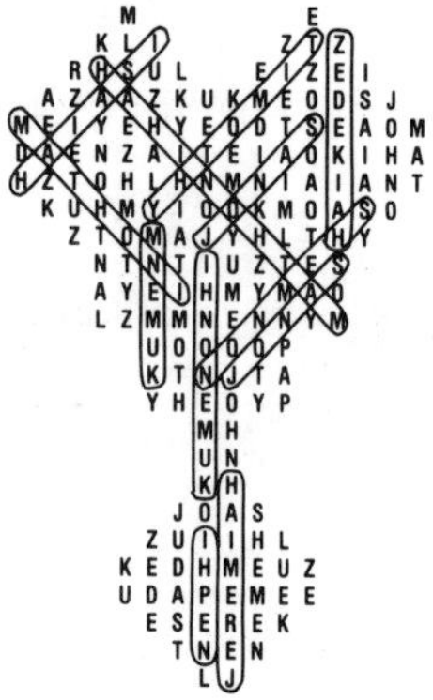

3 Nephi 19:4

NEPHI	TIMOTHY
JONAS	MATHONI
MATHONIHAH	KUMEN
KUMENONHI	JEREMIAH
SHEMNON	JONAS
ZEDEKIAH	ISAIAH

15

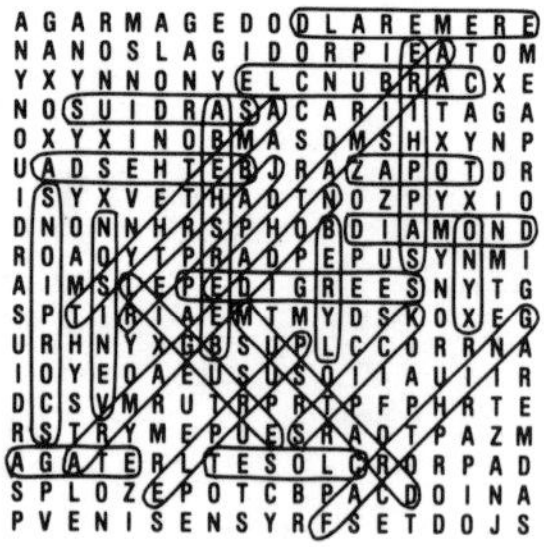

16

PLAIN AND PRECIOUS

City	ARIMATHAEA	Matt. 27:57
Battle	ARMAGEDDON	Rev. 16:14-16
Well of the oath	BEERSHEBA	Gen. 21:31-32
Naval hospital	BETHESDA	John 5:2
Breastplate stones (12)	SARDIUS	Exod. 39:8-13
	TOPAZ	
	DIAMOND	
	BERYL	
	CARBUNCLE	
	LIGURE	
	ONYX	
	EMERALD	
	AGATE	
	JASPER	
	SAPPHIRE	
	AMETHYST	
Sting	SCORPIONS	Deut. 8:15
Blood lines	PEDIGREES	Num. 1:18
Seed	MUSTARD	Matt. 13:31
The uttermost	FARTHING	Matt. 5:26
Into	CLOSET	Matt. 6:6
Deer	VENISON	Gen. 25:28
Of Judah	STICK	Ezek. 37:16
Color	PURPLE	Num. 4:13

17

MIRACLES

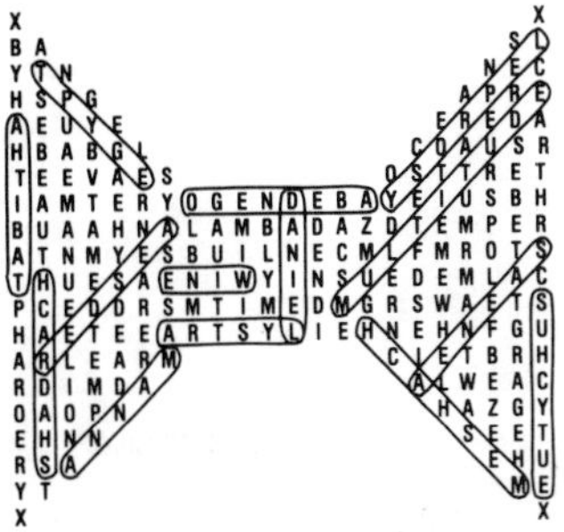

Dan 3:26	Three men in fiery furnace:	SHADRACH
		MESHACH
		ABEDNEGO
Daniel 6:16	DANIEL cast into den of lions.	
Exodus 16:14-15	MANNA sent for food.	
Exodus 10:19	Locusts swept into the RED SEA.	
2 Kings 5:3, 5	Naaman cured of LEPROSY.	
Exodus 7:4	Ten plagues were brought upon EGYPT.	
Acts 20:9	Young man named EUTYCHUS restored to life.	
Acts 14:8-10	Cripple man at LYSTRA made to walk.	
Acts 9:40	TABITHA raised from the dead.	
Acts 9:33	AENEAS cured of palsy.	
Matthew 15:32-39	Feeding the MULTITUDE.	
John 2:9	Water into WINE.	

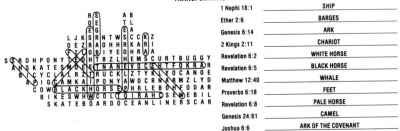

18

VIRTUES

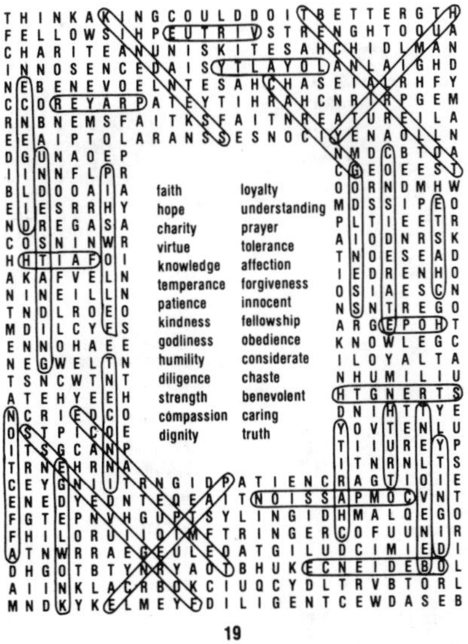

19

TRANSPORTATION

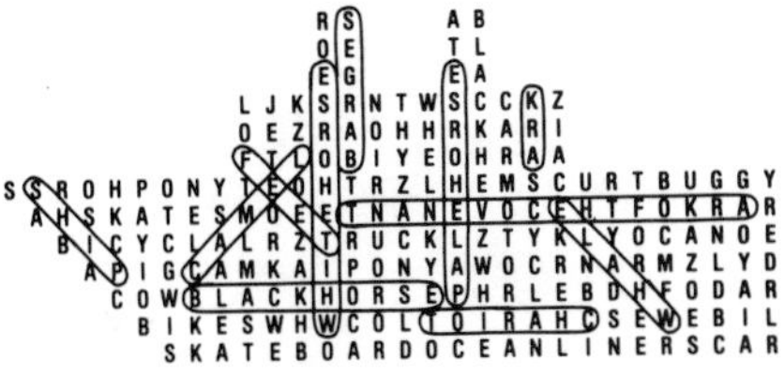

1 Nephi 18:1	SHIP
Ether 2:6	BARGES
Genesis 6:14	ARK
2 Kings 2:11	CHARIOT
Revelation 6:2	WHITE HORSE
Revelation 6:5	BLACK HORSE
Matthew 12:40	WHALE
Proverbs 6:18	FEET
Revelation 6:8	PALE HORSE
Genesis 24:61	CAMEL
Joshua 6:6	ARK OF THE COVENANT

20

BOOK OF MORMON NAMES

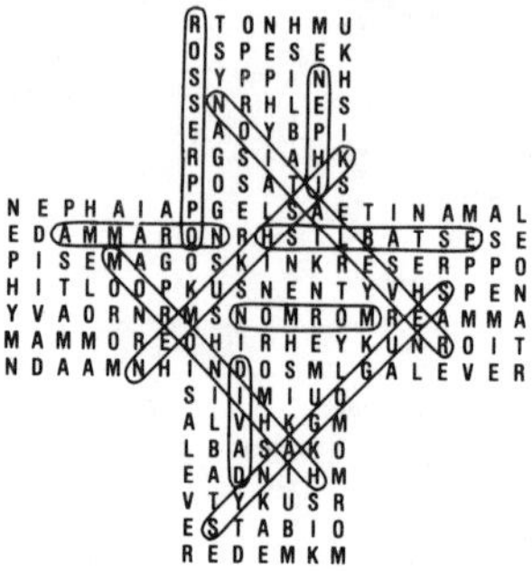

Mosiah 27:13	This is my church and I will ESTABLISH it.	
Helaman 2:5	KISHKUMEN sought to destroy Helaman.	
Alma 45:10	According to the spirit of	REVELATION
3 Nephi 7:17	Great power given to	NEPHI
Alma 32:5	Places of worship	SYNAGOGUES
Alma 62:43	Moroni's son	MORONIHAH
4 Nephi 47	Brother of Amos	AMMARON
Mormon 1:5	Mormon's father's name	MORMON
Mormon 2:5	Driven out of the land of	DAVID
2 Nephi 8:13	And where is the fury of the	OPPRESSOR

21

FAMOUS NAMES FROM THE SCRIPTURES

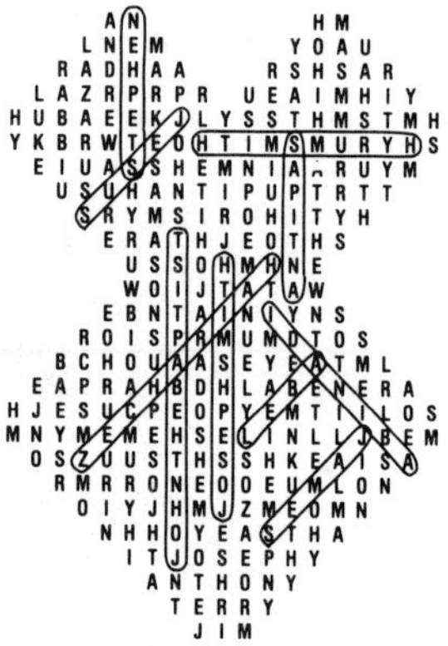

2 Chronicles 24:20-21	ZECHARIAH
Mark 6:24-25	JOHN THE BAPTIST
Matthew 27:50	JESUS
Acts 22:20	STEPHEN
Acts 12:2	JAMES
Mosiah 17:20	ABINADI
D&C 135:1	JOSEPH SMITH
	HYRUM SMITH
Revelation 2:13	ANTIPAS
Genesis 4:8	ABEL

23

HOW MANY BOOKS OF THE NEW TESTAMENT CAN YOU FIND?

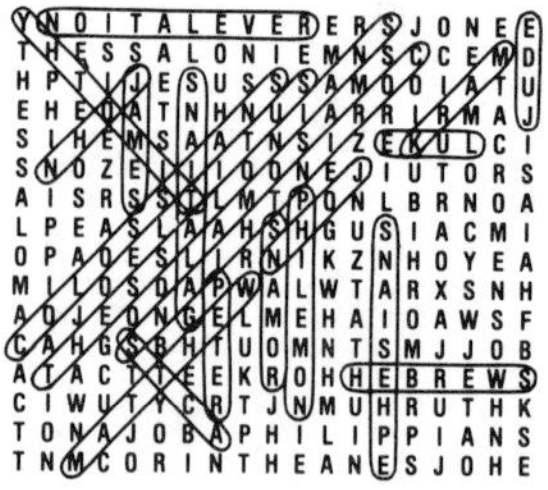

1. MATTHEW
2. MARK
3. LUKE
4. JOHN
5. ACTS
6. ROMANS
7. CORINTHIANS
8. GALATIANS
9. EPHESIANS
10. COLOSSIANS
11. THESSALONIANS
12. TIMOTHY
13. TITUS
14. PHILEMON
15. HEBREWS
16. JAMES
17. PETER
18. JOHN
19. JUDE
20. REVELATION

22

DOCTRINAL THEMES

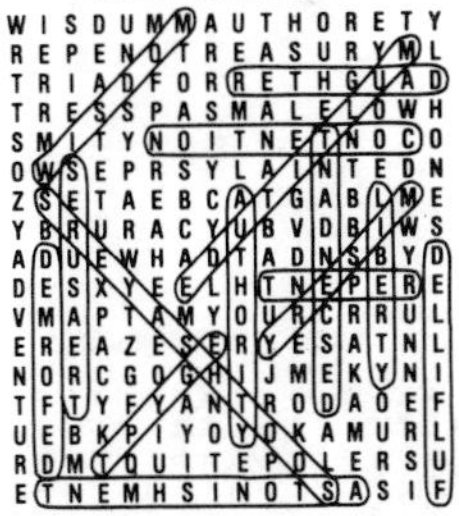

1 Nephi 8:33	And great was the MULTITUDE	
Ether 5:6	For ye shall know that I have AUTHORITY	
2 Nephi 3:4	And I am a DESCENDANT	
Mormon 2:8	They did not REPENT	
2 Nephi 12:6	And hearken unto SOOTHSAYERS	
Helaman 13:19	That they shall hide up their TREASURES	
Alma 2:1	There began to be a CONTENTION	
3 Nephi 15:5	The law in me is FULFILLED	
Alma 62:4	Standard of LIBERTY	
2 Nephi 3:10	Out of the land of EGYPT	
Ether 8:11	The DAUGHTER of Jared	
3 Nephi 10:2	For so great was the ASTONISHMENT	
Alma 32:12	That ye may learn WISDOM	
Helaman 3:29	Gulf of MISERY	
3 Nephi 8:17	The whole earth became DEFORMED	

24

PSALM 23

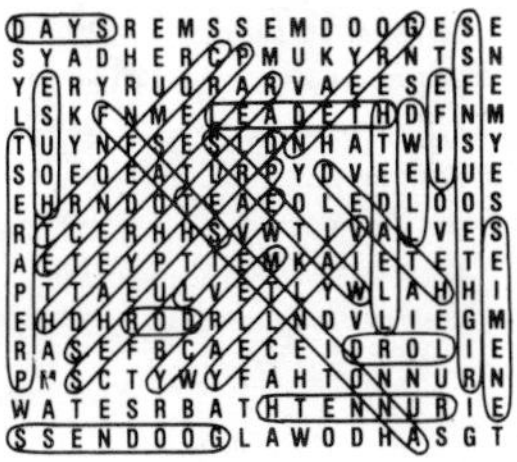

1. The Lord is my SHEPHERD; I shall not want.

2. He maketh me to lie down in GREEN PASTURES: he LEADETH me beside the still WATERS.

3. He RESTORETH my soul: he LEADETH me in the paths of RIGHTEOUSNESS for his name's sake.

4. Yea, though I walk through the VALLEY of the SHADOW of DEATH, I will fear no EVIL: for thou art with me; thy ROD and thy STAFF they COMFORT me.

5. Thou PREPAREST a table before me in the PRESENCE of mine ENEMIES: thou ANOINTEST my head with oil; my cup RUNNETH over.

6. Surely GOODNESS and MERCY shall follow me all the DAYS of my LIFE: and I will DWELL in the HOUSE of the LORD for ever.

26

GOSPEL TERMS

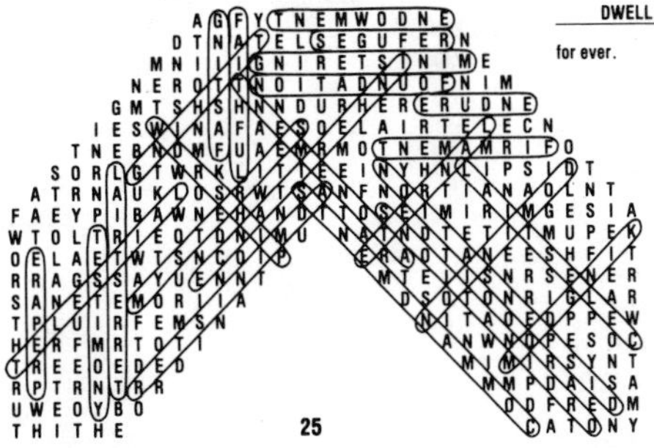

25

MORE BOOK OF MORMON NAMES AND PHRASES

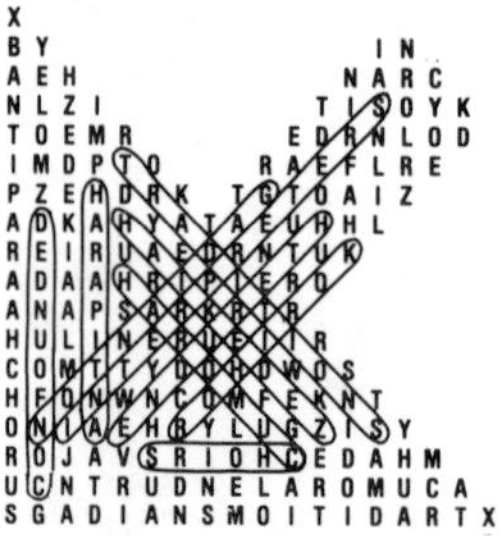

Helaman 7:25	Secret band established by	GADIANTON
Mormon 8:2	Great and tremendous battle at	CUMORAH
Alma 56:34	Strongest Lamanite army stationed at	ANTIPARAH
Alma 38:2	For blessed is he that	ENDURETH
1 Nephi 14:2	Shall no more be	CONFOUNDED
Alma 24:7	And to convince us of the	TRADITIONS
Alma 30:12	Anti-Christ	KORIHOR
Mormon 7:7	Groups of singers	CHOIRS
1 Nephi 1:4	King of Judah	ZEDEKIAH
Ether 4:5	Wherefore I have sealed up the	INTERPRETERS

27

BOOK OF MORMON CITIES

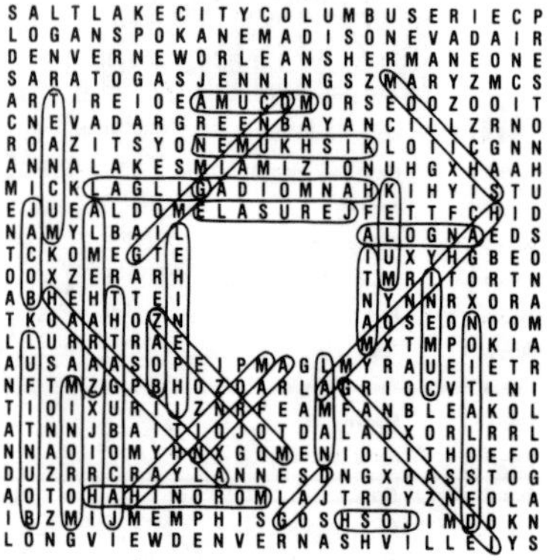

Alma 52:17 (2)
BOUNTIFUL
MULEK

Mosiah 7:21 (2)
LEHI NEPHI
SHILOM

Alma 8:13
AARON

Alma 8:6
AMMONIHAH

Mormon 2:4
ANGOLA

Mormon 4:20
BOAZ

Alma 56:14 (4)
MANTI
ZEEZROM
CUMENI
ANTIPARAH

Mormon 4:3 (2)
TEANCUM
DESOLATION

3 Nephi 9:3-10 (16)
ZARAHEMLA
MORONI
MORONIHAH
GILGAL
ONIHAH
MOCUM
JERUSALEM
GADIANDI
GADIOMNAH
JACOB
GIMGIMNO
JACOBUGATH
LAMAN
JOSH
GAD
KISHKUMEN

28

DO YOU KNOW THE LATTER-DAY PROPHETS? FIND ALL 15 OF THEM.

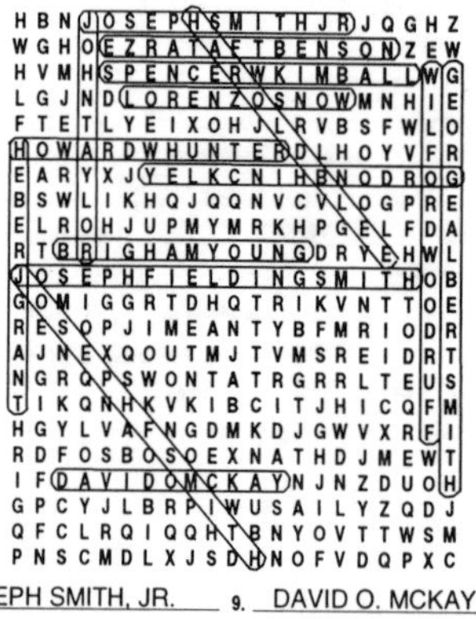

1. JOSEPH SMITH, JR.
2. BRIGHAM YOUNG
3. JOHN TAYLOR
4. WILFORD WOODRUFF
5. LORENZO SNOW
6. JOSEPH F. SMITH
7. HEBER J. GRANT
8. GEORGE ALBERT SMITH
9. DAVID O. MCKAY
10. JOSEPH FIELDING SMITH
11. HAROLD B. LEE
12. SPENCER W. KIMBALL
13. EZRA TAFT BENSON
14. HOWARD W. HUNTER
15. GORDON B. HINCKLEY

30

SCRIPTURE GEMS

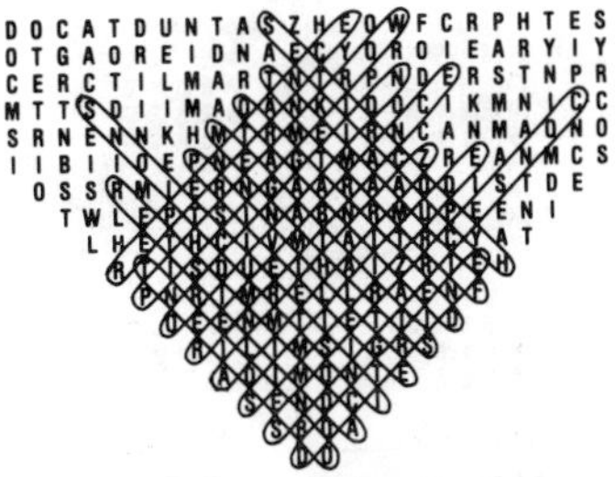

Moses 1:6	And thou art in the SIMILITUDE	
Abraham 4:31	They shall be very OBEDIENT	
Moses 2:6	Let there be a FIRMAMENT	
Moses 7:36	And among all the WORKMANSHIP	
D&C 132:3	To receive and obey the INSTRUCTIONS	
D&C 125:3	And let the name of ZARAHEMLA	
D&C 68:1	Was called by his ORDINATION	
JS—H 2:60	Every STRATAGEM	that could . . .
11th Art. of Faith	We claim the PRIVILEGE	
D&C 83:6	Shall be kept by the CONSECRATIONS	
Moses 6:46	For a book of REMEMBRANCE	
D&C 124:98	From those who would ADMINISTER	
Abraham 4:25	And the Gods ORGANIZED	the earth.
D&C 50:8	But the HYPOCRITES	shall be detected.
D&C 10:62	True points of my DOCTRINE	
D&C 18:6	Stirred up unto REPENTANCE	

31

PRIESTHOOD POSITIONS

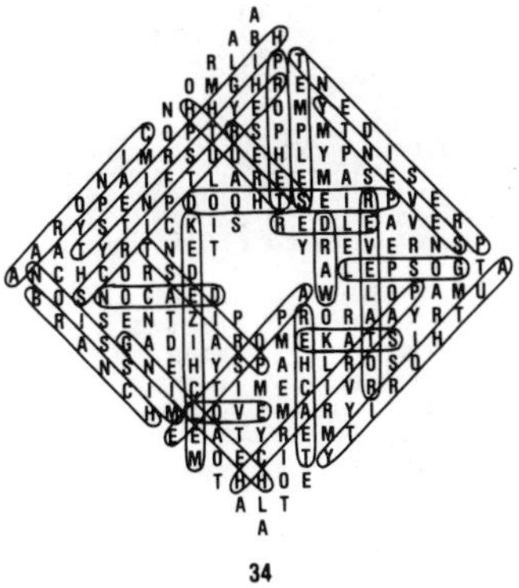

34

A POTPOURI OF SCRIPTURE TERMS

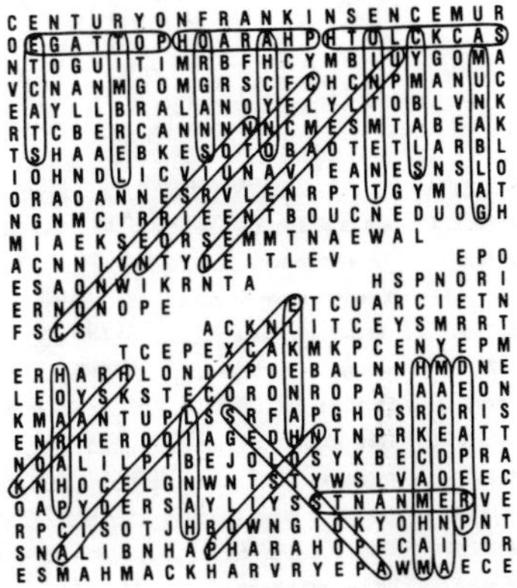

Genesis 37:34	A type of clothing SACKCLOTH
Psalms 150:4-5	Instruments (3) TIMBREL CYMBALS ORGANS
D&C 1:14	Twelve APOSTLES
Exodus 30:34	Sweet spices (3) STACTE ONYCHA GALBANUM
D&C 123:5	Educational volumes ENCYCLOPEDIA
Genesis 41:25	Ruler of Egypt PHARAOH
Exodus 12:15	Without rising agent UNLEAVENED
D&C 113:10	Pieces REMNANTS
Matthew 26:6-7	Oily fragrant substance OINTMENT
Genesis 25:33-34	Birthright sold for POTTAGE
D&C 84:72	Venom POISON
Matthew 8:5	Roman officer CENTURION
D&C 45:61	To be made ready PREPARED
Acts 16:9	A Greek territory MACEDONIA
Acts 15:3	A changing CONVERSION
Abraham 1:6	Evil gods (5) ELKENAH LIBNAH MAHMACKRAH KORASH PHARAOH

32

MORE BOOK OF MORMON TERMS

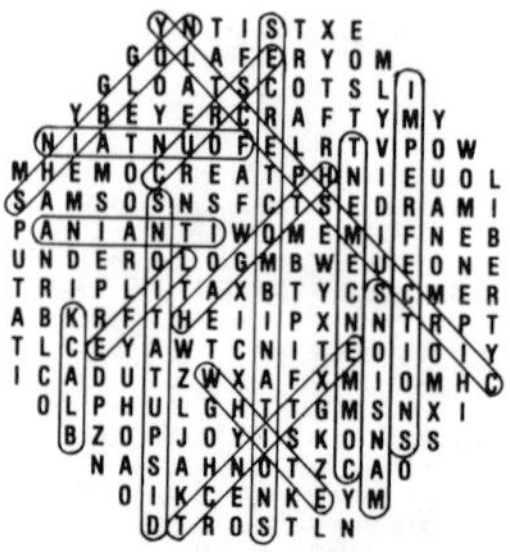

3 Nephi 18:34	No DISPUTATIONS among you.	
Helaman 15:5	And they do walk CIRCUMSPECTLY before God.	
Alma 63:5	Builder of ships	HAGOTH
Mosiah 18:5	Now there was in Mormon a	FOUNTAIN
Alma 21:11	The name of a village	ANIANTI
Enos 27	Prepared for you in the	MANSIONS
Mormon 8:12	Because of the IMPERFECTIONS which are in it.	
2 Nephi 26:22	These will open safes	SECRET COMBINATIONS
Alma 38:5	Alma's son	SHIBLON
Alma 56:20	This comes before graduation	COMMENCEMENT
3 Nephi 2:15	Their CURSE was taken from them.	
3 Nephi 3:8	Until ye shall become	EXTINCT
Alma 5:58	Book of	LIFE
3 Nephi 12:36	Colors (2)	BLACK WHITE

35

PEOPLE, PLACES AND THINGS

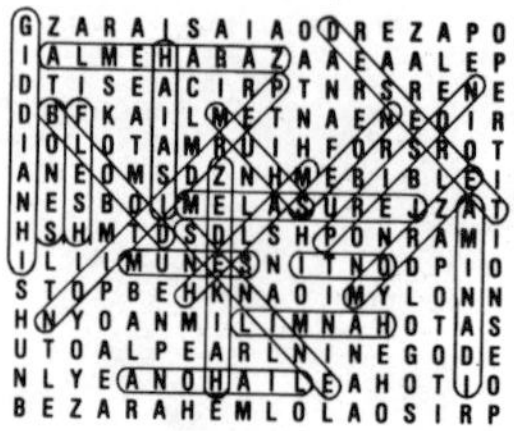

1 Nephi 7:7	Where?	JERUSALEM
1 Nephi 5:12	King	ZEDEKIAH
Mosiah 23:20	City	HELAM
Alma 11:5	Gold (4)	SENINE SEON SHUM LIMNAH
Alma 11:6	Silver (4)	SENUM AMNOR EZROM ONTI
Alma 10:13	Into	PRISON
3 Nephi 27:32	Son of	PERDITION
3 Nephi 16:17	Prophet	ISAIAH
Alma 22:27	Land of	ZARAHEMLA
Mormon 6:15	Body componants (3)	FLESH BONES BLOOD
Alma 37:38	Compass	LIAHONA
Alma 10:2	Interpreted	AMINADI
3 Nephi 3:9	Governor	GIDDIANHI
Ether 2:3	Honey bee	DESERET

36

DOCTRINES FROM THE DOCTRINE AND COVENANTS

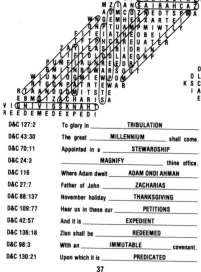

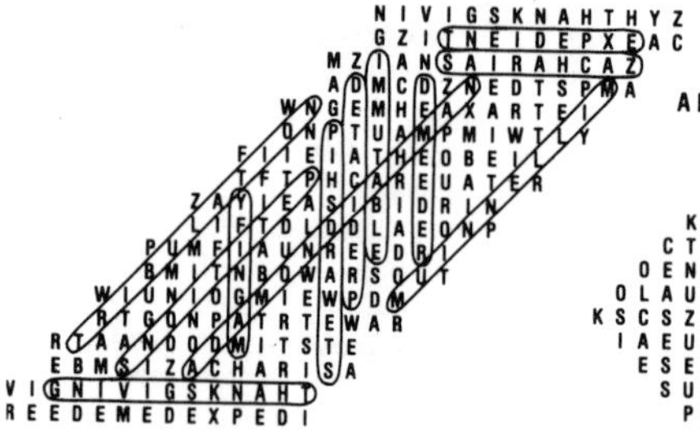

D&C 127:2	To glory in	TRIBULATION
D&C 43:30	The great MILLENNIUM shall come.	
D&C 70:11	Appointed in a	STEWARDSHIP
D&C 24:3	MAGNIFY thine office.	
D&C 116	Where Adam dwelt	ADAM ONDI AHMAN
D&C 27:7	Father of John	ZACHARIAS
D&C 88:137	November holiday	THANKSGIVING
D&C 109:77	Hear us in these our	PETITIONS
D&C 42:57	And it is	EXPEDIENT
D&C 136:18	Zion shall be	REDEEMED
D&C 98:3	With an IMMUTABLE covenant.	
D&C 130:21	Upon which it is	PREDICATED

37

A FEW THINGS MISSIONARIES SHOULD HAVE

KNOWLEDGE	BICYCLES
REFERRALS	HOLY GHOST
DESIRE	SUBSISTENCE
SCRIPTURES	KNEEPADS
FAITH	COMPANIONS
ENDURANCE	MAPS
TESTIMONY	MONEY
PRAYER	STUDY

38

HOW GOOD ARE YOU?

Try finding the words in this puzzle without turning the book around.

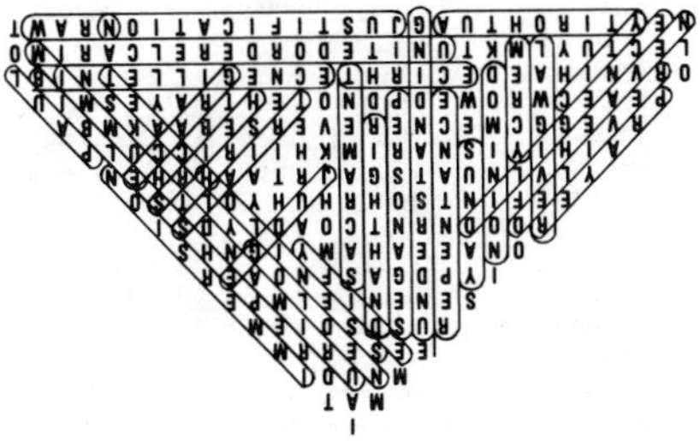

39

VIRTUES AND BLESSINGS

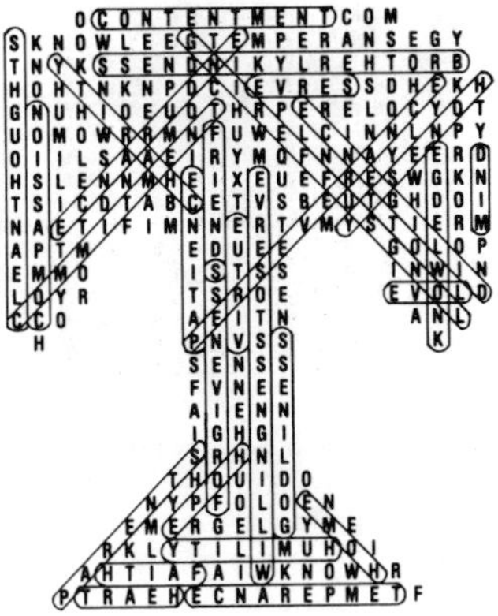

WE MUST HAVE:

D&C 4:6 (11) FAITH, VIRTUE, KNOWLEDGE, TEMPERANCE, PATIENCE, BROTHERLY, KINDNESS, GODLINESS, CHARITY, HUMILITY, DILIGENCE

D&C 84:41 FORGIVENESS

D&C 64:2; 3 Nephi 17:7 COMPASSION

WE MUST ALSO HAVE:

endurance ● longsuffering ● love ● perseverance ● honesty ● hope clean thoughts ● willingness to serve ● commitment

AND WE ARE INDEED BLESSED IF WE HAVE:

loving PARENTS, caring FRIENDS, a happy HOME, a sincere HEART, a desire to SERVE.

IF WE POSSESS ALL OF THE ABOVE, WE WILL HAVE:

peace of MIND and CONTENTMENT.

40

Z WHAT YOU CAN DO WITH Z'S

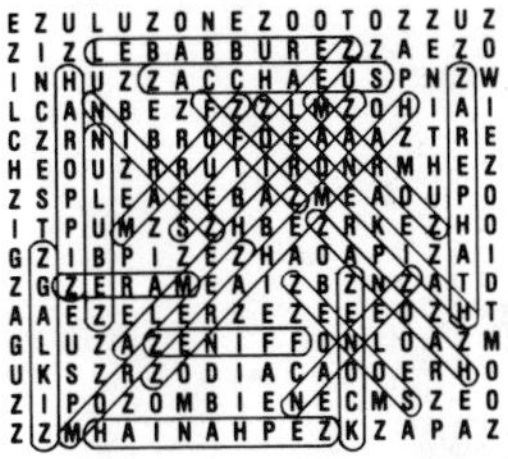

1 Kings 17:9	City where Elijah dwelt	ZAREPHATH
Alma 10:31	A lawyer	ZEEZROM
Exodus 2:21	Wife of Moses	ZIPPORAH
Mosiah 7:9	Grandfather of Limhi	ZENIFF
Ezra 2:2	Also known as Sheshbazzer	ZERUBBABEL
Alma 16:5	Chief captain	ZORAM
Luke 6:14-15	Simon and others called	ZELOTES
Mosiah 11:8	Precious metal	ZIFF
2 Kings 25:18	Second Priest	ZEPHANIAH
3 Nephi 10:16	Two prophets	ZENOS ZENOCK
Joshua 15:31, 34, 37	Cities (3)	ZIKLAG ZANOAH ZENAN
Alma 43:5	Leader of Zoramites	ZERAHEMNAH
Genesis 30:20	Son of Jacob and Leah	ZEBULUN
Alma 2:22	A spy	ZERAM
Luke 19:2-5	Climbed a tree to see Jesus	ZACCHAEUS
3 Nephi 8:8	City	ZARAHEMLA
Jeremiah 49:34	King of Judah	ZEDEKIAH
1 Nephi 4:35	Servant of Laban	ZORAM
Ether 12:30	Mountain	ZERIN

42

NEW TESTAMENT TEACHINGS

Luke 21:28	Your REDEMPTION draweth nigh.
Revelation 1:11	I am ALPA AND OMEGA.
Ephesians 6:4	Bring them up in nurture and ADMONITION.
John 21:16	FEED my sheep.
Matthew 6:4	That thine ALMS may be in secret.
Titus 1:7	For a BISHOP must be blameless.
1 Peter 3:11	Let him ESCHEW evil.
John 21:15	FEED my lambs.
Matthew 5:3-11	These are called the BEATITUDES.
Acts 27:7	We sailed under CRETE.
2 Corinthians 5:7	For we walk by FAITH, not by sight.
Mark 5:34	DAUGHTER thy faith hath made thee whole.
Hebrews 2:3	If we neglect so great SALVATION.
Acts 23:11	So must thou bear witness also at ROME.
John 6:71	He spake of JUDAS ISCARIOT.
1 Timothy 3:12	Let the DEACONS be the husbands of one wife.
Galatians 3:1	O foolish GALATIANS.
Luke 20:9	And let it forth to HUSBANDMEN.
Matthew 19:14	SUFFER little children.
John 21:10	Bring of the FISH.
Revelation 3:16	So then because thou art LUKEWARM.
John 11:25	I am the RESURRECTION.
Matthew 6:13	Not into TEMPTATION.
2 Thessalonians 2:8	And then shall that WICKED be revealed.
John 21:17	Jesus said unto him, FEED my sheep.

44

FIND 26 KINGS IN THE BOOK OF MORMON

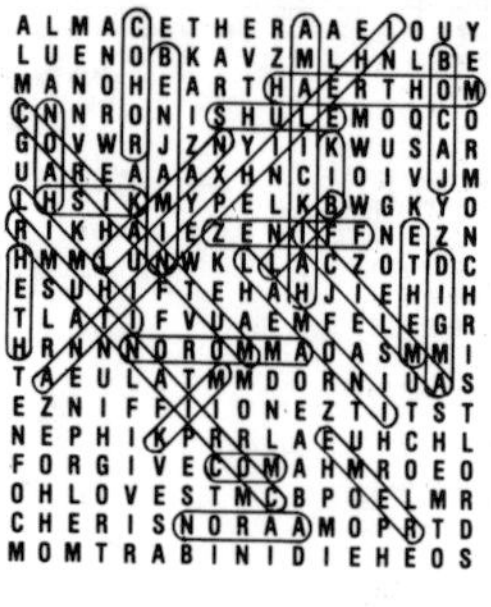

Mosiah 11:27	NOAH	Omni 24	BENJAMIN
Mosiah 19:29	LIMHI	Alma 17:21	LAMONI
Mormon 2:9	AARON	Ether 10:32	COM
Alma 2:9	AMLICI	Alma 47:35	AMALICKIAH
Alma 52:3	AMMORON	Alma 24:3	ANTI NEPHI LEHI
Ether 10:32	AMGID	Ether 7:15	SHULE
Ether 7:20	COHOR	Ether 9:21	CORIANTUM
Ether 9:21	EMER	Ether 12:1	CORIANTUMR
Ether 11:11	ETHEM	Ether 10:30	HEARTHOM
Ether 9:26	HETH	3 Nephi 7:9-10	JACOB
Ether 7:3	KIB	Ether 10:13	KIM
Ether 10:17	KISH	Ether 10:18	LIB
Mosiah 7:21	ZENIFF	Mosiah 7:21	LAMAN

46